Jets

Kate Riggs

seedlings

CREATIVE EDUCATION • CREATIVE PAPERBACKS

Published by Creative Education and Creative Paperbacks
P.O. Box 227, Mankato, Minnesota 56002
Creative Education and Creative Paperbacks are
imprints of The Creative Company
www.thecreativecompany.us

Design by Ellen Huber
Production by Chelsey Luther
Printed in the United States of America

Photographs by Corbis (Peter Adams, Eddy Joaquim/
Spaces Images, Pete McBride/National Geographic Society),
Dreamstime (Carlosphotos, Iulius Costache, Brett Critchley,
Robwilson39, Pablo Scapinachis, Yaro75), Getty Images
(Giovanni Colla/Stocktrek Images, Tyler Stableford),
iStockphoto (Estate of Stephen Laurence Strathdee),
Shutterstock (Sylvie Bouchard, egd, Brian Kinney, Luminis,
Tatiana Popova, pzAxe, Carlos E. Santa Maria)

Library of Congress Cataloging-in-Publication Data
Riggs, Kate.
Jets / Kate Riggs.
p. cm. — (Seedlings)
Summary: A kindergarten-level introduction to jets,
covering their speed, pilots, role in transportation, and such
defining features as their pointy noses.
Includes index.
ISBN 978-1-60818-521-4 (hardcover)
ISBN 978-1-62832-121-0 (pbk)
1. Jet planes—Juvenile literature. I. Title. II.
Series: Seedlings.

TL547.R574 2015
629.133'349—dc23   2014000182

CCSS: RI.K.1, 2, 3, 4, 5, 6, 7;
RI.1.1, 2, 3, 4, 5, 6, 7; RF.K.1, 3; RF.1.1

First Edition
9 8 7 6 5 4 3 2 1

TABLE OF CONTENTS

Time to fly!

Jets are fast
airplanes.

They can fly
high in the air.

The main part
of a jet is the
body. A jet
has two wings
to help it fly.

The front of a jet is pointy.

It is called the nose.

A pilot flies the jet.

The pilot sits in the cockpit.

Small jets hold one to five people. Jumbo jets carry hundreds!

A jet takes off from an airport. It flies above the clouds.

Go, jet, go!

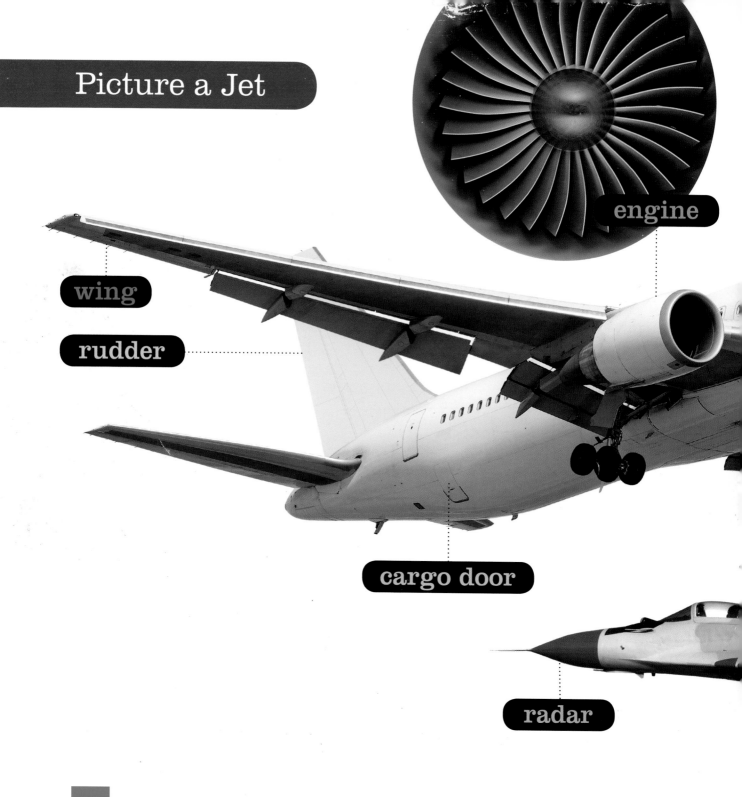

Picture a Jet

engine

wing

rudder

cargo door

radar

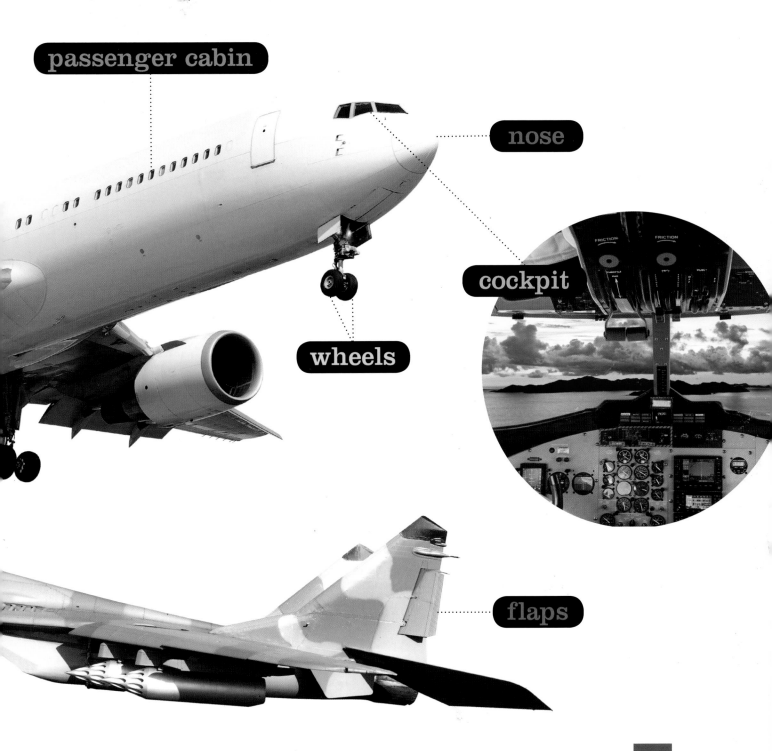

passenger cabin

nose

cockpit

wheels

flaps

Words to Know

cockpit: the place where an airplane pilot sits

pilot: the person in charge of a jet

jumbo: a very large airplane

Read More

Lindeen, Mary. *Airplanes*.
Minneapolis: Bellwether Media, 2007.

Ridley, Frances. *Speedy Jet Planes*.
Mankato, Minn.: New Forest Press, 2010.

Websites

Letter J Jet Printable Activities
http://www.first-school.ws/activities/alpha/j/jet.htm
Keep learning about jets, with the help of fun activities.

Military Coloring Pages
http://www.supercoloring.com/pages/category/military/
Print out pictures of fighter jets to color.

Index